COACH

MY WORLD AND GET THE HELL OUT OF IT!

THE WIT AND WISDOM OF

HAYDEN FOX

AS TOLD TO

Barry Kemp, Judd Pillot, and John Peaslee

HYPERION NEW YORK

Photos courtesy of: Gale M. Adler, Frank Carroll, Bob Coburn, Bonnie Colodzin, Bob D'Amico, Chic Donchin, Jerry Fitzgerald, Rory Flynn, Len Hekel, Craig Sjodin, Bob Nese, Randy Tepper, Ron Tom.

COACH: My World and Get the Hell Out of It!
The Wit and Wisdom of Hayden Fox as told to Barry Kemp, Judd Pillot, and John Peaslee, based on the Universal Television series "COACH" created by Barry Kemp.

Library of Congress Cataloging-in-Publication Data
Kemp, Barry.
    Coach : my world and get the hell out of it! : the wit and wisdom of Hayden Fox /
  as told to Barry Kemp, Judd Pillot, and John Peaslee. — 1st ed.
      p.   cm.
    ISBN 1–56282–765–0
    1. Coach (Television program). 2. Football—Humor. 3. American wit and humor.
  I. Pillot, Judd. II. Peaslee, John P. III. Title.
  PN1992.77.C55K46 1993
  791.45'72—dc20   93–8099
                                                CIP

First Edition

10 9 8 7 6 5 4 3 2 1

Design, incidental illustration, and production by Robert Bull Design
Photo page 12: Tim Davis/Photo Researchers

CONTENTS

COACH

FOREWORD

When the good, kind, wonderful, beautiful people at Hyperion approached me about writing a book (and told me I'd be paid by the word), I couldn't have been more excited, ecstatic, thrilled, impassioned, atingle, aroused, or inflamed.

I immediately said, "Yes, absolutely, sure, why not?"

After all, being an educator, I've always found books very useful. I think my respect for books began when I was a small boy. I used to stack them on top of each other in order to climb up and reach my father's *Playboy*s. It's for that reason that books still excite me. I only hope this book is thick enough to be of use to some young lad or some short grown man.

So the question now becomes, "What does Hayden Fox write a book about?" They asked me to write what I know. Obviously, you can't write a book about everything and yet they've given me a whole one hundred pages, so why not try? So call this the preamble, the pre-statement, the foreword, the frontispiece, the what-have-you to *My World and Get the Hell Out of It!*

By the way, you may be wondering about the title. If you're like me, you probably feel this way a lot. You have a view of the world that is clear, consistent, and totally out of step with everyone else's. But hey, everybody's got their own stupid opinions. That's what makes America a great planet.

So here it is, the world according to me in one hundred glorious pages. I hope you enjoy this book very, very, very, very, very, very, very, very, very, very, very, very, very, very, very, very...

much.

(Only 98 pages to go.)

FOOTBALL

I chose the subject of football for my first chapter because football is a lot like life, only a lot more fun. Life can be a struggle. So can a football game. (Unless you're playing William and Mary or the Oglethorpe Stormy Petrels or some other wuss team.) But while you can never completely win at life, you can win at football. (Unless you're playing Notre Dame or Miami or some other out-of-control team.)

I've said many times, I was never as happy as the day Kelly was born or the day we won the Pineapple Bowl. But while I frequently forget Kelly's birthday . . .

. . . I will never forget December 25, 1991, in Honolulu, Hawaii.

There are so many things I love about college football. The idea of taking a young, awkward, underdeveloped seedling of a boy . . .

. . . and turning him into a warrior, is enormously gratifying.

(Especially since I find young, awkward, underdeveloped seedlings really annoying.)

But watching young men grow is only one of the satisfactions of coaching at the college level. Watching young cheerleaders grow is yet another satisfaction.

There is an electricity to a crisp autumn afternoon at a college football game. At Minnesota State, sixty thousand fans descend on our little school to scream, wave their banners, and drink Beaver Beer. (A local brew made from pure Minnesota lake water. For the more health-conscious, they also make Beaver-Lite. For the insanely health-conscious, they make a non-alcoholic beer, appropriately called "Dam!")

I awake in the pre-dawn hours before every game with an unbelievable adrenaline rush. I just can't wait to get to the game. I can't even sit still long enough to eat breakfast, so I have a steak-and-egg sandwich and a pot of coffee in the car. From the moment the first fans come through the kiosks, until the last Porta Potti is loaded onto the flatbed trucks at day's end, I'm in my glory. Pacing the sidelines like a wild cat, barking instructions like a wild dog, I don't know what's beating louder—my heart or the drums from the Screaming Eagle marching band. I just know I feel like I'm going to explode . . . and it's joyous. My biggest fear is knowing it can't go on forever. Someday I'm going to be retired, and short of swallowing a stick of dynamite every Saturday, I don't know how I'm going to get this rush again.

When I leave football, I'm going to leave behind a lot of great memories.

The pomp and circumstance . . .

the camaraderie . . .

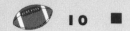

the post-game victory celebrations . . . .

But most of all, I'll miss my great friends, Keith Jackson and Bob Griese, whom I met for three minutes once after a Penn State game.

But enough of this talk of leaving football. I'm never leaving football. It's my life and it's going to be my death. As you can see, I've already picked out my final resting place.

It's the field position I most enjoyed: Deep inside enemy territory and well within field goal range. Unfortunately, it's my last down. Now on to life.

CHAPTER 2

HAYDEN FOX ON

LIFE

As much fun as football is, it only takes up about three quarters of your time on this earth. The rest of that time is spent playing another little game I like to call life. This is a much more confusing game than football. Everybody makes up their own rules, and where you really need protective equipment, you have none.

People have been trying to figure out life for eons, but especially since "Donahue" came on. We all have so many questions about life: Where do we come from? Where do we go when we die? Where should we eat? And these are just the most common ones. There are literally a dozen more.

But I think life gets a little easier to understand if you're a football coach, because life is a lot like a football game. Moment by moment, play by play, hit by hit, you're trying to figure out . . .

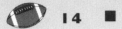

whether you're winning . . .

. . . or losing.

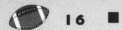
I'm usually losing.

But the truth of the matter is, you never know until the game is over whether you've won or lost. The only thing you can hope for while you're alive is that you score as often as possible.

I consider the big score in my life to be Christine.

We've scored 1,306 times. (Don't tell Christine I told you this.
This is the kind of stat she considers intimate.)

Once you've scored enough so that you don't have to go around bragging about it, there's the rest of life to contend with. Unlike football, where you get to play one position for most of your career, a person will assume many different positions over the course of his or her life. (Here I'm not talking about scoring.) You'll play student/teacher, child/parent, husband/ex-husband, reader/author. But in life, no matter what position you play, you will always be on the defensive.

On the following page I have included an excerpt from an interview I did for the student newspaper at Minnesota State, the *Screaming Eagler*. (Or "the Squawker" as I call it.) It's from a column they run, "Profiles On Campus." I understand this was widely reprinted so you may already have read it. In the interview, I answered some questions about life. Although this was published over a year ago, in rereading it, I see my views haven't changed.

THE SCREA**M**ING EAGLER

PUBLISHED FREQUENTLY ON THE MINNESOTA STATE UNIVERSITY CAMPUS SINCE 1987

PROFILES ON CAMPUS: Coach Fox

by **CUBBY INGVAT**

Q: Do you believe in God?

A: I had my doubts up until this year's Pineapple Bowl. But now I do.

Q: What's the most important lesson you've ever learned?

A: My old college coach, Jake Connelly, once told me, "There are few things in life more important than a good friend. They are: a clear conscience and a fuzzy memory."

Coach Hayden Fox

Q: After you're gone, what would you like to be remembered for?

A: Do you mean after I've gone to another university or after I'm dead?

Q: After you're dead.

A: I guess I would like to be remembered as a person of great integrity, great humanitarianism, great leadership, and someone who never cared about any recognition for himself. In fact, if they ever name a building after me, I'd like that on the wall.

CHAPTER 3

HAYDEN FOX ON

INTIMACY

Most men have trouble being intimate. (I'm talking emotionally, not sexually. Let's face it, a man would make love in a supermarket if he were asked. But try to get him to talk about his real feelings and he'll be in that express lane and out of the market before you know it.)

I think this inability to talk about things like feelings probably dates back to caveman times when men were the hunters and women were primarily cooks and cave cleaners. Women had a lot of time to swap recipes and bones for their hair and talk about their cave guys. Men, on the other hand, had to keep quiet so they didn't scare off dinner. This set a pattern that has only begun to change in recent years. Men now are expected to not only kill dinner but to have feelings and to talk about them. Although this has been personally a painful transition for me, I have really come to believe in those moments of intimacy between two people, and I'm really happy to share mine with all of you.

Looking back at all the moments in my life, I think the ones where
I've really felt close to another human being have
been the warmest and most
memorable.

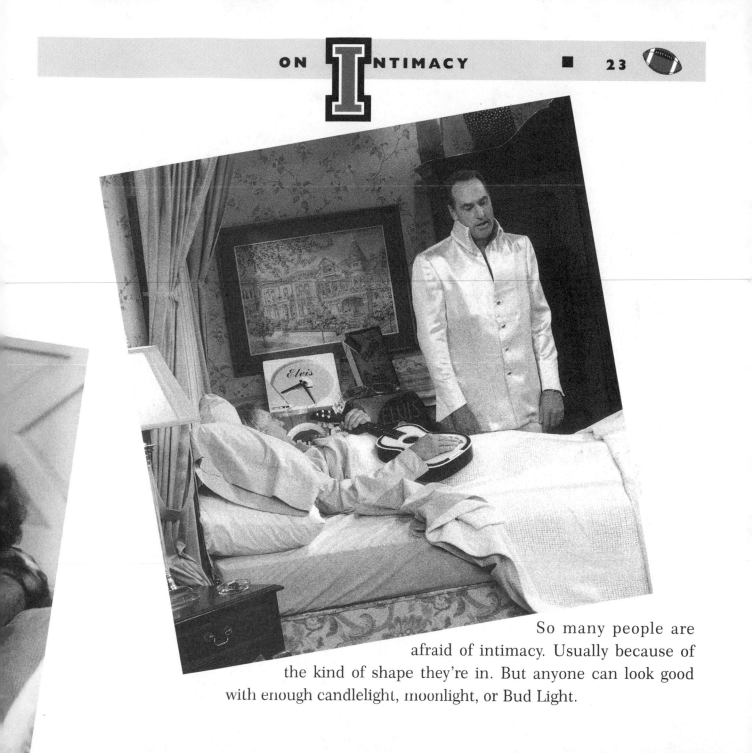

So many people are afraid of intimacy. Usually because of the kind of shape they're in. But anyone can look good with enough candlelight, moonlight, or Bud Light.

The keys to being intimate and enjoying it are: A) be honest about your feelings, and B) have someone to be intimate with. Anybody can be intimate alone. I really think being intimate with another person is the key here.

Sometimes it's harder to be honest with people we know well. That's why being intimate with a complete stranger is not a bad place to begin. Let's say you're in a supermarket or a bar. You're waiting in line for the butcher or for the pool table. You could say to the stranger in front of you, "That's a lovely piece of meat you've chosen," or, "Are those your balls?" You have taken the first baby step toward being intimate with another person. Eventually, you'll be able to have intimate conversations with people you know. And possibly, someday, even with people you love.

CHAPTER 4
HAYDEN FOX ON
LOVE

First of all, understand that despite my seemingly gruff though somewhat roguish exterior, at my core I'm a hopeless romantic. I don't think there's a more beautiful word in the English language than the word "love," but it runs the risk of being devalued through overuse. Americans use the word to describe everything from their feelings for God to deodorant. "I love my Lord" is perfectly acceptable. "I love my roll-on" is unacceptable. The word should only be used to express a sacred emotion that is deep, intense, ultimate. For example:

I love Christine.

I love football.

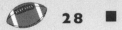

I love steak.

I love animals.

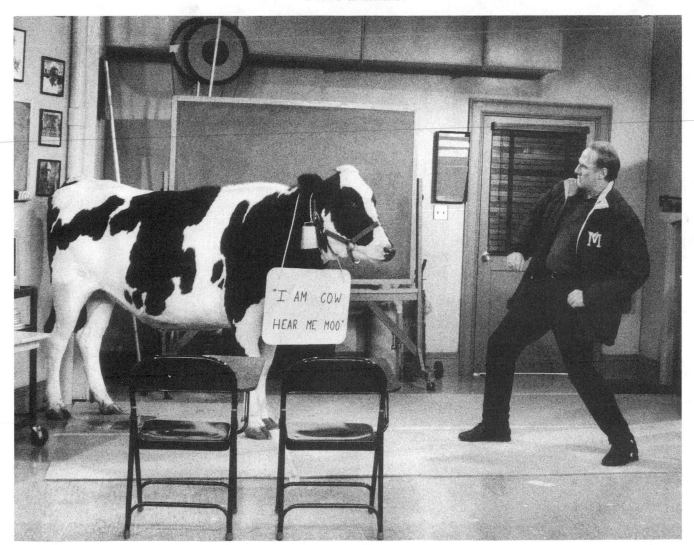

But do I love all of these things the same? No. I do not love animals as much as I love Christine, football, and steak. Unless the animal can be made into a steak or a football. (I hope this is not offensive to animal-rights activists. Before you get upset, I'm the one who insisted they not put a fur cover on this book.)

Luther loves animals, too. Every year on the first day of hunting season, he puts on this moose hat and runs through the forest as a decoy, trying to help the other moose get away.

You may still have questions about when it's appropriate to use the word love and when it is not.

The following is a list of things that I feel are appropriate "to love":

Things that are not appropriate "to love":

Your parents	A book
Your country	A cat
Your lover	A suit
Your kids	Women's basketball
Your car	Art
Your hometown	War
Your team	Musicals
Susan Sarandon	Flavored coffee
Your job	Mimes
Your God	Bagpipes
Your life	Foreign films
Your publishing company	New York

Hopefully, these lists will be helpful in determining how to live your life.

CHAPTER 5
HAYDEN FOX ON ART

I wasn't going to include this as a chapter, but my daughter, Kelly, being in the arts (whatever the hell that means) insisted I include at least a few words on the subject. What can you say about art that won't bore people to tears? I've never understood it, and I'm proud to say I've never bought any of it. The only things I would even consider hanging in my house are those sports pictures by Leroy Neiman-Marcus, but I understand those are very expensive. And I'm not about to throw away a couple hundred dollars on something I can see in any hotel bar. Nevertheless, in order to please my daughter, I include here my lists of the kinds of art I like and the kinds of art I don't like.

The kinds of art I like:

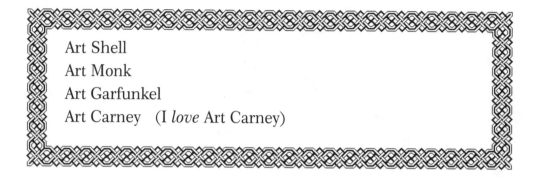

Art Shell
Art Monk
Art Garfunkel
Art Carney   (I *love* Art Carney)

The kinds of art I don't like:

The Expressionists
The Impressionists (Except Rich Little. I *love* Rich Little.)
The Cubists
Stu-art

CHAPTER 6
HAYDEN FOX ON
FOOD

O ne of the perks of being a big-time college football coach is getting to travel throughout these blessed United States and dining in fine restaurants on the university's money.

Unfortunately, because I'm a big-time college football coach, I'm frequently recognized and hounded for autographs or else berated for my team's performance. Therefore, I sometimes am forced to don a disguise.

On the following page is my list of the top five culinary experiences in America and my personal rating for each one:

= *A restaurant so bad even Luther wouldn't eat there. None exist that I know of.*

= *Usually tasteless food in small portions. French restaurants, health food restaurants, most California restaurants.*

= *Usually tasteless food, but with huge portions. Most of your smorgasbords and cafeterias.*

= *Great food, huge portions, short dresses on the waitresses.*

= *All of the above, plus they know me and make a big deal of it when I come in.*

Now put on a bib, because when you read this list, you're going to start drooling all over this book.

The Touchdown Club

Minnesota State University.
Slabs of beef the size of a boot, and so rare you can milk them. For you health freaks, excellent fried chicken.

The Pork and Cork

(Formerly *The Wine and Swine.*)
(Formerly *The Hog and Grog.*)
Chattanooga, Tennessee.
Chops so big the fat sometimes hangs off the table and dangles onto your knee.

The Beef Bowl

Midland, Texas.
Chili so spicy it'll make your eyes water just standing in line. Even the next day when you walk down the street, people know you've been to The Beef Bowl. Even next week, when you get back to Minnesota, people will know you've been to The Beef Bowl. In fact, once you've been there, people will always know you've been to The Beef Bowl.

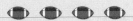

Jake's Steaks

Tallahassee, Florida.
A little pricey, but well worth it when you consider the pound of pintos that comes on the side.

Mom's

Mobile, Alabama.
Everything is batter-dipped and butter-fried. It tends to be a younger crowd, but that's because the cholesterol has killed most of the older crowd. Nevertheless, a great way to go. ("Mom's" would be a solid four footballs because the skirts are short here too, but unfortunately, Mom's the one who wears them. Consequently, she loses half a football every five to ten years.)

While all of these restaurants are mouth-wateringly delicious, sometimes a man likes to treat himself to a home-cooked meal. And sometimes when Christine's not home, I have to cook it myself. Over the years, I have managed to come up with a recipe or two that, at the risk of sounding immodest, are better than anything you'll eat on the world's two continents.

One of these is "Fox's Famous Five-Alarm Chili." If any of you gals want to, you can even cut this out and put it in your little recipe box. Here it is:

FOX'S FAMOUS FIVE-ALARM CHILI

1 wheelbarrowful of shredded beef
   (the U.S.D.A. grade does not matter)
1 pillowcaseful of red beans
1 tomato
2 pints of Tabasco sauce
1 size eight sneakerful of horseradish
A generous handful of cayenne pepper
A drop (and I do mean just a drop) of kerosene

Note: A nice glass of pilsner is the perfect complement to this meal. If at all possible, try to track down a case of Beaver Dark

My other favorite recipe, perfect for a Sunday brunch or a midnight snack, is "Señor Zorro's Huevos Rancheros." (*Zorro* is Spanish for fox. I don't know what the hell *huevos rancheros* means.) The ingredients are:

> *Exactly the same as the Five-Alarm Chili except you whip up a wheelbarrowful of eggs.*

Beverage Note: A better complement than beer for this dish is champagne or a screwdriver. As always, do not drive and eat these eggs.

CHAPTER 7
HAYDEN FOX ON SEX

After a big meal, whether it be pork, beef, what have you, a man is ready for a little "dessert." (I assume the same is true for you gals because I'm not doing it by myself.) There are many different kinds of sex. There is sex with your wife, there is sex with women who are not your wife . . . Actually, that's all I can think of. Let me say right now that I believe in safe sex. No matter who I've been going with, I have always been monotonous. However, to keep one woman interested over a long period of time, a man has to remain tender, sensitive, and above all, romantic. One way to remain romantic is to have a favorite romantic spot. I may be a little overly romantic, but I have five favorite spots. They are:

Behind the ear
Under the arm
Anywhere on the neck
The back of the knee
The back of the car.

Regardless of your favorite spots, there are basic steps you must take to get to them. The following are the five steps to what I romantically refer to as "pay dirt":

#1. CHAMPAGNE

Tastes like crap . . .

. . . works like a charm.

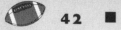
#2. DANCING TO SOFT MUSIC

Any song by Frank Sinatra will do.
(If you've had enough champagne,
any song by Frank Sinatra, Jr., will do.)

#3. ROMANTIC FIRELIGHT

Especially effective if your date is not as pretty as Christine. Or if you're battling a cold sore.

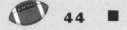

#4. THE KILLER LINE

Did anyone ever tell you you look like a stewardess?

or . . .

Are you as sweaty as I am?

Unless you're a complete nimrod, by now
you've swept her off her feet.

You have hit . . .

#5. . . . PAY DIRT

She'll be like putty in your hands.

Note: If none of this works, do what Luther does—get a bird and a dog and try to forget about sex.

CHAPTER 8

HAYDEN FOX ON

CHRISTINE NUDE

(turn the page)

Oh, yeah. Like I'm going to show Christine nude. What are you, an idiot? Go to Chapter 9.

CHAPTER 9

HAYDEN FOX ON

THE FAKE

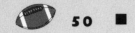

You've just experienced it. Go to Chapter 10.

GETTING TO THE TOP

I've only been on top for a short while, so this is going to be a short chapter.

Nobody gets to the top without a philosophy, and one way to get a philosophy is to borrow one from people who have already gotten to the top.

The late great coach George Allen once told me:

"Hit hard and watch the good things happen."

I don't know what this meant, but it was great having my picture taken with George Allen.

Another football great, Hall of Famer Johnny Unitas, once said to me:

"Head straight for the goal line and don't look back."

I think what he meant was, if you have a dream and you believe in yourself, go for it and don't let anyone tell you you can't do it.

I've lived by that motto more than once.

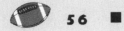

And finally, the great coaching legend, Hank Stram, winner of Super Bowl IV with the Kansas City Chiefs, once said to me at a coaches conference in Memphis, Tennessee:

"Hayden, I think you've got my suitcase."

I think what he meant was, all coaches carry similar emotional baggage. But it's how you carry it that separates the greats from the not-so-greats. At least I hope that's what he meant. If that's not what he meant, then it's a heck of a coincidence that Hank and I wear the same size shorts.

But it wouldn't be fair to talk about being on top without acknowledging that every coach spends some time at the bottom.

Depending on who's on top, being on the bottom doesn't have to be a bad thing.

But if you're talking football, being on the bottom is awful. (And I'm not talking about being a player and being on the bottom of a pile. That can actually be fun. I've had some fairly interesting conversations while I waited for the officials to pull eight guys off my back and someone's cleat out of my nose.) But if you're a coach, being on the bottom is hell. The fans hate you, the alumni hate you, and most of all, you hate yourself. The only people who like you are the other teams in the league, but you hate them.

Although the past few seasons have seen me riding high and becoming in the words of . . . well . . . me, revered, I've had more than my share of losing. From small schools in Florida to places like Chattanooga and Akron, I've had to coach some of the biggest misfits ever to stumble onto a football field.

There was Carl Funderman, a 148-pound linebacker who didn't discover until the last game of the season he was playing on two right cleats.

Victor Di Stasio, whose nickname was "Victim," a weak-armed quarterback from New York City who, every time he got blitzed, threw his wallet and watch at the opposing linemen in hopes that they'd stop.

And then there was our kicker, Jan Stuudenborg, or "Stupidborg," as those of us who hated him called him, who could only kick while smoking.

A lot of coaches might have quit given "talent" like this. But I kept going because I love the game of football, and I never wanted to teach gym again. Fortunately, I persevered and triumphed. But for all you coaches out there who have yet to taste the sweet fruits of victory—who have yet to experience the rush of being lifted on your team's shoulders after a great win—I can only say, "Stay with it and keep trying. There are better days ahead! (Unless you're over forty. Then I'd get out and become a bartender. You'll still get to talk sports and watch sports all day long, and you'll be doing it with people who are even bigger losers than yourself.)"

HAYDEN FOX

ON

FAMILY & FRIENDS

The following pages are from my personal scrapbook. I include them for two reasons: One, they say a man is measured by the friends he keeps and the family he makes and I wanted to show you how I stack up, and two, these pictures take up a lot of pages.

This is a picture from the night Christine and I met.

You can't actually see us but we're in the flatbed.

This is a picture of me and Luther. Luther is my best friend and has been for over twenty years, but I can honestly tell you in all that time, this is the only time I've seen him in his underwear.

This is Dauber after he shaved his head. The guys on the team told him they'd all do it if he did it first. He did. They didn't. He was disillusioned.

This is the night my daughter, Kelly, walked back into my life after sixteen years. I was shocked because the last time I saw her she was sucking on a piece of zwieback toast.

This is the night Kelly walked out of my life and married her beloved Stu-art. Afterward, everyone left and I sucked on a piece of zwieback toast.

This is the day Kelly walked back into my life, after her beloved Stuart dumped her. We both would have killed for a piece of zwieback toast.

This is a picture of zwieback toast.

This is Kelly today. The turmoil she has come through in her life has brought us closer. In fact, with each passing day, she becomes more and more the son I never had.

This is a picture of Christine meeting my ex-wife, Beth, for the first time. We were at the Touchdown Club. While Beth is not technically family, she's had a big impact on my life, and she is the mother of my ~~son.~~ daughter.

Here I am at a typically festive holiday gathering.

This is another picture from the same festive holiday gathering.
These are Stuart's parents. Goons extraordinaire.

This is a picture of me during the annual Fox family reunion. Each year, the whole clan gets together in a different part of the country for a weekend of warmth, good times, and reminiscing. No matter where it's held, I always call in to say hello. This is what family is all about.

*Here I am at another family gathering; the first time I met Stuart.
I really do enjoy being around my loved ones, and I hope I can find
a picture in here where I'm smiling.*

Here's one of me about to smile. Of course, you can't see where Christine's hands are in this picture, so all bets are off.

There's been a lot of talk in recent years about families and family values. I forget by who. But it's led me to do a lot of thinking. When I was a young man, I didn't know why I would ever want a family. They're expensive, time-consuming, and emotionally draining. (Except for the emotional part, they're a lot like your first car, and I got rid of that as soon as I could.) But now that I'm older, I've come to appreciate the importance of family. I still find them expensive, time-consuming, and emotionally draining, but there's nothing like the feeling of knowing that you can be the biggest jerk in the world and somebody still loves you. They may not talk to you for a couple of years at a time, but they still love you. And let's face it, it's also nice to know that when it's time to meet your maker, somebody you love will be there to pick up a shovel.

CHAPTER 12

HAYDEN FOX ON

COLLEAGUES

After your family and friends, the people you have to put up with next are your colleagues, but at least you get paid for this. Some people are both colleagues and friends. I understand Clinton and Gore are close. Siegfried and Roy live together, I think. I'm lucky to have my own Siegfried and Roy, Luther and Dauber.

These guys are not only great pals, they're great coaches.

They are unbelievably loyal, incredibly hardworking, and surprisingly wily tacticians. Here they are helping to pour the floor for my game room.

Luther has been my best friend for so many years that this book wouldn't feel right without Luther having his own special section. That's how important he is to me. The following paragraph is devoted exclusively to my buddy, Luther Van Dam.

My Buddy Luther Van Dam

The first time I saw Luther was my first day of college football practice. I was a gangly, gawky, freshman running back, and Luther was the backfield coach. Right away he was different from the other coaches. There they all were with their chests stuck out and their whistles in their mouths, barking commands. And there was Luther with his stomach stuck out and a Bavarian creme in his mouth, wiping custard off his jersey. I took an instant liking to him. Through four years and a Tangerine Bowl victory (and I don't know how many doughnuts), we became the best of friends. When I got my first head coaching job, I hired Luther as my top assistant. He's been with me ever since. But he's more than just my assistant coach. Sometimes he acts as my father, sometimes my brother, and sometimes my six-year-old son. But not a day goes by that I don't think back to that first time we met and wonder what life would have been like if I had taken to one of the other coaches. Buddy, this one's for you.

I also want to say a few words about my other good buddy,

Michael "Dauber" Dybinski

I first heard about Dauber when he was a senior at Herbert Hoover High School in Rupert, Idaho. (Or maybe it was Herbert Rupert High School in Hoover, Idaho. I don't really remember.) What I do remember is writing and asking him to send me some films of him playing. He sent home movies of when he was five playing in a wading pool in his back yard. While this misunderstanding caused me some concern (how dumb was this guy?), I was impressed that a five-year-old could stand in four feet of water, and only have it come up to his knees. I thought, "this was a young man who might just be big enough and good enough—and have the academic standards—to fit in at Minnesota State." I was correct on all counts.

Dauber has probably grown more in the ten years I've known him (I'm speaking intellectually) than any player I've ever coached. Today, after eight years of college, three different majors, and a diploma, Dauber represents what a young man can do when he has determination, perseverance, and financial aid. I know it's a cliché to say this, but in this case it's a true cliché; I wish I had a hundred more like you, Big Guy.

This book would not be complete (nor would it be one hundred pages) if I didn't include some of the other people that I work closely with. On the following pages are photographs of some of my esteemed colleagues, as well as University President Elaine Tewksbury and Band Director Riley Pringle.

Here I am in a discussion with University President Elaine Tewksbury. She's making some point or other.

Here is Athletic Director Howard Burleigh, letting his hair down. (Ha-ha.) We were at a football-equipment convention in Las Vegas. After attending for five minutes, we thought we should treat ourselves to some fun. Howard is dancing with the internationally acclaimed Chevalier girls. (*Cheval* means "horse" in French.) Guess what part of the *cheval* Howard is playing?

Here I am with Band Director Riley Pringle discussing the half-time show. It was a salute to "Batman," but we couldn't get the rights to the costume. Fortunately, Mrs. Pringle, a whiz with a needle and thread, whipped up this dandy costume for Riley just in the nick of time. Unfortunately, most people thought we were doing a salute to "The Mummy."

Here I am discussing Kelly's academic progress with one of her dance instructors from the University.

Here I am in another discussion with University President Elaine Tewksbury. I played college football for four years and suffered cracked ribs, two knee injuries, and a pulled groin, but I never took an aspirin until I met this woman.

Here is a picture of women's basketball coach Judy Watkins, show-ing Dauber how to do "The Watusi." She may actually be a real Watusi. She is also Dauber's fiancée, which means I have to be nicer to her than I normally would be, which means I can only call her a Watusi in a book. I couldn't say it to her face. In fact, to say anything to her face you'd have to be as tall as Vlade Divac.

Speaking of Vlade Divac, I am throwing in a picture here just to show I know him, too. I also know Rick Barry.

See? And I even touched him.

Here again is Athletic Director Howard Burleigh. We were all in Hawaii for the Pineapple Bowl and Howard heard about it and tried to join us. Fearing he would hurt morale, I had him arrested.

Here again is University President Elaine Tewksbury. She must have been making a point but, for the life of me, I can't remember what it was.

And finally, here is a picture of my beloved secretary of ten years, a woman who has put up with more than any human could be expected to withstand, my dear, dear Mrs. Thorkelson. (I can't remember her first name.)

CHAPTER 13

HAYDEN FOX ON

HUMOR

In conclusion, let me say a few words about humor. Humor is one of the essential elements of life. I think this, too, probably goes back to caveman times. They may have been prehistoric but they weren't pre-hysteric. (See? Humor.) I think you can tell a lot about a person by what he thinks is funny.

For example, I think this is . . .

Funny!

This is <u>not</u> funny.

DUNK

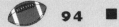

Funny!

Not funny.

Funny!

What do you think?

If you think this is funny, you've misunderstood the whole chapter on humor.

Here I am on page 98 of this book. Only two more pages to go until I fulfill my contractual obligation.

Here I am on page 99. Boy, this has been quite a journey. Six hours ago I thought I'd never get here. But I did and I thank you for reading it. Hopefully, you've learned something and felt whatever you paid for the book—be it ten, twenty, a hundred dollars—was worth it. I know it was for me. I have saved the best picture for last.

The author wishes to thank the following people
for their support and help with this book:

Erin Wilkey
Lynn McCluggage
Jon Vandergriff
Elaine Essex
Julie Jackson
Universal Television
ABC Television Network
MCA Publishing Rights
The entire staff, cast, and crew of COACH
and
The heedfully solicitous and benevolent gentlepersons
at Roget's Thesaurus.

The author also wishes to thank his three dear collaborators
(whose names he can't remember), without whose help, vision, wit,
and intelligence this book could not exist. (Nor could I.)

The End

Note to Hyperion:
This is technically an extra page. Do I get a bonus?

For a free "COACH" cast photo
and information on "COACH" merchandise,
please write to:
"COACH" Collectibles
Building 78
100 Universal City Plaza
Universal City, CA 91608